P9-AFM-763

Waiting for Poppa
at the
Smithtown Diner

POEMS BY
Peter Serchuk

WAITING FOR POPPA
AT THE
SMITHTOWN DINER

UNIVERSITY OF ILLINOIS PRESS

Urbana and Chicago

Publication of this work was supported in part by a grant from
the Illinois Arts Council, a state agency.

© 1990 by Peter Serchuk
Manufactured in the United States of America
P   5   4   3   2   1

This book is printed on acid-free paper.

Grateful acknowledgment is given to the following magazines in which these poems,
some in earlier versions, first appeared:

The American Poetry Review: "For Poppa, Asleep in the Smithtown Madhouse"
Ascent: "Driving through Canada"; "For the Woman Whose Sister Is Dead"; "Counting
   Fingers"
Epoch: "Tired of the Road"
Green House: "New Letters from Uncle Vanya"
The Hudson Review: "Night Song"; "Bar Harbor: For a Moment by the Water"; "Bent
   Tree"; "Last Words at Marblehead"; "Summer on Green Lake"
The Indiana Review: "Waiting for Poppa at the Smithtown Diner"
The Kansas Quarterly: "The Children Must Come"
Manhattan Poetry Review: "For My Brother: On the Courage of Birds"
Mid-American Review: "The Long Nights of Waiting"; "In the Attic Where She Sleeps"
The Missouri Review: "A Note Found after the Storm"
New Letters: "A Christmas Card from Wyandotte, Michigan"
The Paris Review: "What the Animals Said"
Poet & Critic: "The Angel on the Backyard Porch"; "Looking Out from Herring Cove";
   "A Papal Mass at Auschwitz Forty Years after the Holocaust"
Southwest Review: "The Woman in the Dream"
Sou'wester: "A Blue Vase with White Chrysanthemums"

Earlier versions of some of these poems were part of a manuscript that received first
prize in the University of Michigan's Hopwood Awards in 1974. "What the Animals Said"
also appeared in *The Hopwood Anthology: Five Decades of American Poetry* (1981).

The author wishes to thank the executive directors and the trustees of the
Corporation of Yaddoo.

Library of Congress Cataloging-in-Publication Data
Serchuk, Peter, 1952–
    Waiting for Poppa at the Smithtown diner: poems / Peter Serchuk.
      p. cm.
    ISBN 0-252-06104-7 (alk. paper)
    I. Title.
PS3569.E68W3 1990
811'.54—dc20
                                        89-5065
                                        CIP

For my brothers Fred and Steve,
and for Michele

The herrings are awake.
What's all the singing between?
Is it with whispers and kissing?

Theodore Roethke

CONTENTS

I

NIGHT SONG

There were no words.

Just the pie we'd left by the fire
for the coons, the half-moon curled
yellow in the sky, a cold breeze sliding
along the side of the warm tent.

Inside, within the goose down bags,
my hands were as dark as the places
they slept in and the deep clean lines
touched more than they could know.

She whispered something I have now
forgotten; something about dying
in a place where no one would find you,
within dark woods or white waves.

We loved the night in the changing air
and in the morning woke early to watch
the sun sweep across from tree to tree,
lifting the damp from the open leaves.

BAR HARBOR: FOR A MOMENT BY THE WATER

For a moment, with the lights turned off in the beach house,
you confused the rocking of cradled water with my rhythmic
    breathing
and carefully lifted the blankets from my body.

The room was still as a summer leaf, and only the breeze
through the window moved within, scurrying like a cat
under the bed, under the desk, over the chair.

I lay quiet with my lids shut tight, feeling your cautious eyes
slide over my chest, across my thighs, along my legs,
scanning the dark edges of flesh hair, my only cover.

I did not speak as you touched my side, touched my face,
your warm hand bringing blood to my cheek, resting
like a bluebird on the contour of my forehead.

You became motionless in the intuitive silence, and it was then
that I fell asleep, dazed, thinking how the sun rises slowly
these mornings, pacing itself like a runner above the white
    Maine coast.

And I can touch you now, strangely dropping back to that same
    sleep
of silent vertigo and feel my pulse lead me to objects beyond
    my hands,
far far removed, barely within the reach of words.

DRIVING THROUGH CANADA

Love, where is this car taking us? My hands
are on the steering wheel but I'd swear it has
a mind of its own. The fog is thick in the Ottawa

air and the rain on the windshield
leaves the footprints of small animals dancing
in the woods. Should we live in this car for good?

Our radio plays only love songs and each time
I tap my foot we pass another truck. Even the turn
signals keep beat with the music! We could raise

a flock of kids in the back seat and teach them
the different road signs. At night they could take
the wheel in shifts and find secret routes to nowhere,

to Buffalo! All of our answers would be circled
on maps, they'd be there in the glove box should we
ever forget. We'd sleep to the hum of the engine and wake

in some truck stop to buy coffee and a chocolate bar—
The road to Toronto can't be very far!
Say you want to drive. I'll write letters to our friends.
To say we're passing through, to say we've just arrived.

At Frost's Grave

Nothing savage moves here.
In June faith is the patience of lilac stems
More silent than sleeping birds.
The field mouse turns its face to the shade.
Rain worms hug the cool stones.
All trust is soft breathing.

Summer in Bennington
And even the dead can't stop themselves
From dreaming. Even-tempered now
The great poet Frost sleeps here.
Family man, the world no longer tempts him
Nor his wife who purrs like a sofa cat
Nor his children who live the long life
Only the heart can imagine.

Unlike love
Or those words ink will not master
This is the world you can set your watch to.
The sun begins its slow walk in Brattleboro
And sets in Hoosick Falls.
Clear mornings rock themselves in sugar maples.
Here heaven finds a saint
For each new nightmare.

Aspen, Colo. (AP) — The frozen body of a young woman,
discovered near here Monday, has been positively
identified as that of a registered nurse from Michigan . . . .
the cause of death has not yet been determined . . . . the
body had been "chewed by animals" and appeared to
have been moved from its original location "probably
by animals," the sheriff said.

1

She was not so sweet as you would think.
Not in the damp of her hair, not in the joint of her bones.
So far beyond sleep, legs spread in the cold,
A stench so foul rose up from her flesh neither
Wolf nor bear had dared to touch her.
The blue eyes and soft feet were not what you remember.
It's better to forget.
The air itself had recoiled from her blood.

2

What brought her here we can't say,
Though perhaps kindness. She carried no weapon.
Also, she was not alone.
They walked together, in whispers, their feet
Packing the wet snow into small cakes.
His steps were large and his voice deeper.
We followed their feet past alder trees,
Past the blackberry stems which are so sweet in summer.

We followed them down to a clearing
And hid in the brush. They spoke louder.
She walked more quickly. He walked faster and grabbed
Her arm. She twisted away. He caught her again
Holding her waist. His hands were thick and his knuckles
White as snow. She screamed, we became frightened.
She screamed, we clawed at the ice. She screamed,
We raced away toward the deep woods.
We heard her screams trail off like a gunshot.

3

You must believe he loved her.
He loved her more than hope, more than pain.
The facts speak for themselves:
He had been so lonely, so terribly lonely, and you too
Know what loneliness will do to desire, what desire does to love.
You too have wanted her.
His loneliness ached him beyond all need. Her body breathed
In the space of her clothes. He touched her
And the smell of pine rushed through his nose like fire.
He wanted her but she refused. It had been too long.
He touched her face. She screamed.
He kissed her neck. She screamed.
It had been too long. He wanted her but she refused.
He never wished her harm.
The facts speak for themselves:
He only wanted her as you.

4

It was quiet for a long time.
The light turned twice and it had snowed again.
We were hungry. It is hard to hunt in snow
And the wolverine is fast on ice. We were hungry and still
She was there. We could smell her blood push through the air
Above the trees. The air was sick. We could barely sniff the pines.
We scratched a path across the woods another time but
It was different from before. She was alone and didn't move.
Also, her clothes were gone and her blue skin stiff. She didn't twitch
When we jabbed her thigh. We took small bites.
Her flesh was tough and hard to chew. We took small bites.
We pulled her back into the thick and turned to go.
The wind was cold against our fur. We were hungry,
But the air was sick.

5

It was a hunter who finally found her.
Searching for bears he'd had no luck. He vomited twice
Behind a bush and dropped his gun. Later, they gathered
Her up into a bag for the walk back home.
"The most disgusting thing I've ever seen," one policeman said.
"You could stick your fingers clear through her cheeks."
The animals slept throughout the day,
Each in its own familiar place.

6

Tell us what repulses you dear Human.
Tell us what frightens your children in their sleep.
Is it the rough claws and coarse teeth? Tell them
To stop crying in their beds. We are only a nightmare.
Their soft feet and tender eyes are safe.
We are not human.

7

Whoever here would die for love, let them pray
To die so blessed. I can't waste tears on her facelessness,
I can only mourn the kindness she never knew.
She knew only our kindness, the hunter's kindness.
If whole now she might tell us how it is to be a part
Of necessity: How the final test of love
Is not in the giving but in the taking.
Be gentle with her bones. The animals
Are running through the woods listening.
Let us bury her alongside all other lovers.

A Blue Vase with White Chrysanthemums

This is no abstract idea.
No inverse argument told conversely.
No bleeding confession of a tortured heart.
No song you sing in your sleep.
This is a blue vase with white chrysanthemums.

The suffering of your eyes is at end here.
The dead will not speak to you in dreams.
The people you love will not leave you lonely.
You will not see nor hear what you have not seen nor heard.
This is a blue vase with white chrysanthemums.

COUNTING FINGERS

When I count the fingers on my hands
twice, the numbers are never the same.

This holds true whether I count by twos,
count by threes, group in fives or slide

each inside my pocket as it's named.
They are indivisible. Sometimes it's a thumb

curled inside my palm or an index finger
gone to call my wife. They refuse to be

defined. They want to run loose beyond my
eyes, crawl into places I'm afraid to look,

to feel things I'm afraid to touch. They
demand a life of their own beyond my wrist,

a life not routed by strange arteries or
protruding veins, not dependent on the breath

of blood. They mock me when I stare at my feet,
at my face, at everything as helpless as my thoughts

and laugh when I examine their abandoned joints
in the light. They know I can't tame their touch.

They know I can only follow.

A Song for Her Skin

Call her a swan. Call hers the skin
of a rose. Say that it's endless
to all who would know and they'd know.
Where it ends is where it begins.

Through long wintery nights I slept
Under curls that fell to her spine.
More than once I slept, more or less.
Her lips in the dark measured mine.

Her neck was as soft as the breath
of a leaf, her mouth the soft heart
of a clam. I called my fingers
fools for not knowing where to start.

Those nights when ice held fast to trees
twisted like old bones in the wind,
she'd arch her back across the sheets
to have me whisper through her knees.

If she sighed while she slept I'd wake
to her sigh. If I leaned my head
closer she'd kiss me in her sleep.
My skin listened to hear hers speak.

HER FAITH

She gives her thoughts to clouds,
Her love to willful men.
Convinced of no God she keeps
Her heart in this heaven,
In a world this perfect.

For the Woman Whose Sister Is Dead

1

For a moment my face reminds her
of the room they shared, of the one long bed
and the small windows looking out on the empty yard.
Embracing, she holds my ears like precious shells
but her eyes are away, wild as blushing orchids.

She remembers her now, as always, before the crash, before
the phone call that turned twenty years into an all-night vigil
   of dust.
She shakes in my arms, her fingers outstretched and stiff.
I pull her closer. I say my name over and over in a slow chant.
I kiss her full-mouthed as only a lover or sister dares.

2

With men it's always been the same.
Behind her eyes she wonders who to love, wonders
if she'll ever let go enough to trust the living.
She flutters like a nuthatch between two trees.
When they offer her promises she knows they'll be broken.
When they offer their bodies she knows they'll never be as soft,
never be as delicate or smooth as the one skin she knew
   completely.
She is repulsed by all that is not gentle.

3

The arguments of her senses cannot be dissected into logic.
She is continually drawn to open spaces, empty fields
where everything is seen except what hides in grass.

Yet always in dreams she returns to woods where two girls
have set a cage-trap for a fox. One is plump and round-faced.
The other small and thin with bony fingers and legs
that stick out from under her school dress like furry twigs.
Late afternoons they're crouched behind trees.
She remembers the goose bumps, the cold toes and blue lips.
She remembers slipping off their pants to pee in the bushes.
At night the long talks and deep dreams become clear
as the moon. The empty yard is forever turning white.
Half of everything she remembers is that November.
She returns to embrace what nothing can change—
Two girls dancing around a baby fox, light snow falling
above their heads, the warmth of each other's skin and the
    love
of animals keeping them happy in a Michigan wind.

      4
She loves me because I know how to keep secrets,
because I've learned not to whisper what ears don't need to
    hear.
So years had passed and nothing was the same. When they
    spoke
it was about men, about work and the summer rainstorms in
    Brazil.
Their letters were the geography of new places.

But when that car slid off the road reckless as any bull
the years began to count themselves backwards. What was
    became
what had been. While one closed her eyes on the fading moon
the other went to sleep in their narrow room dreaming of
    winter.
What they buried later she didn't care to remember.

I'll let others untie the knots of her passion.
She loves me because I know how to keep secrets.

        5
Slowly she returns to our room, returns
to our moment like a child stepping into water.
She is cautious with the air she breathes,
taking my hands to make sure we're alone,
releasing a sigh into the feel of my face.

In a long kiss she says the only thing she can.
Through love I've learned to translate her need.
No matter how many drunk drivers she sees in my eyes
we go on from here; I taking only what she'll risk.
Entwined, we move one night closer together.

THE CHILDREN MUST COME

For Joe Salerno

The children must come.
There's nothing we can do to stop them.
The children must come and they must grow
Larger and larger
No powder bones, no soft teeth.
My friend, the needing is ripe.

The children must come one by one
A generation of strangers.
They must come and they must age us
Make us wise with fear, strangers ourselves
Suddenly aware of what's become
Of our once-young hearts.

The children must come, yes they must come,
If not to say we've failed
Then only to say we've tried long enough.
They must come as we came, in a gentle fury
In a passion we knew
Before love became a passion of logic.

Listen.
Above the sirens and the sawmills you can hear
The thunder of kicking feet.
Shaped in blood the children must come
Insistent on love, insistent on a vision
Beyond a broken heart.

The children must come as they have always come
Night prowlers in our dark street
Shattering our windows with their impatient screams.
The children must come without knowing how the world still
    suffers.
We have no choice but to accept them.
To let them help us.

POEM FOR HIS PREGNANT WIFE

1

Not even you could have known my life.
The childhood I swallowed, my bellyful of shame.
Cripples taught me love and crippled I learned
The geometry of want that maimed their lives.
Now they're dead in the past like everything else.
I take my lessons from visiting ghosts.

2

For each chance of rain and each glance of sun
the seed makes a vow: Deep in the mud-suck
Every breath will be taken. Awkward
In middle-age I wrestle with such faith
Time and again confuse our love with
Changing weather.

3

I call on love to strike a passion out of
Patience, to shape a ripe and budding soul
From pure desire. Oh sister, watching your belly
Float against the moonlight I struggle with
Nothing, I lift the window and fill our room
With the sweet, uncluttered obvious:
The heart of a child will race toward summer.
The grace of God may lift us someday.
The ghosts we fear in the inevitable darkness
Are more often than not squirrels snapping twigs
Under the giant shadows of trees.

A Christmas Card from Wyandotte, Michigan

For Mel Foster

This happens every year you know.
They hang a wreath on the gate to Diamond Chemical
though no one cares and the late shifts
can't see it anyway. It's just as well.
The sky above the plant is green at sunrise
and the tank cars clack all night,
their bellies full of insecticide and antiseptic.

Meanwhile at River Rouge the news is bad.
Car sales are slow. Shifts could be cut.
Five thousand more may have to walk next week.

In the Oak Cafe where everyone loves his wife
but hates to go home, Frank and Zeke stare down
sweet Audrey's dress dreaming of easy answers.
Who can blame them? Everything they build is
being recalled and she floats like some ivory cloud,
a flawless design of moving parts.

God knows they'd like to take her home.
God knows they'd like to lay her good, to tell
this goddamn world they've got something to say
worth listening to. She brings them another drink.
They nod, side-glancing her nipples.
God knows they'd like to take her home.

Someone's put a quarter in the jukebox.
The music howls like a bloody face,
        a harmony of screams and twangs.

Just once I'd like to kill someone.
Not kill them dead but just enough to say
I told you not to fuck with me. That's how
it is when you pray to the patron saint
of smokestacks, when even the sun
wipes its fat face and gets back on the line.

Another one for Frank and Zeke on me!
It's time to go. Time to call my wife
and let her know how Santa loves her.
Outside it's cold and in the propane light
of Mr. Diamond's plant the white flakes look
like blue leaves falling from heaven.

Peace on earth. Goodwill toward men.
I'd like to tie that sweaty wreath around his neck.
My wife's gonna kill me for getting drunk again.

WINTER POEM

The wounded season is over.
This is the quiet I've listened for.
Raw winds gnaw the brittle stems, white flakes
Rise up like sparrows from the dead grass.
I teach myself where the barbeled carp
Sleeps beneath the ice.

1

In late afternoon, alone on the beach,
We watch the red sun make its way down to the water,
Gliding endlessly, it seems, like the herring gulls
Who squawk above our heads.

The ocean too glides smooth along the sand,
Covering the cove again with its cold salt blanket.
From the cliffs distant boats seem half in the sky.
We bid them calm winds and kiss to the privilege of being
    in love.

2

Come morning, with the tide out,
We walk inside the cove to dig for clams
And search for shells. Instead,
We find foot-long shads and alewives lifeless
In the sun, gills too breathless to chase the moon,
Their silver sides and blue backs dried out in the open heat.

Closer to the tide-line there are even menhaden,
Once secret to the perfect corn of the Narragansetts.
Munnawhatteau, they called them: *He fertilizes.*
The word and the deed were one and the same.
I think of this as we examine each fish,
Remembering those words we whisper for love.

What a cruel and perfect world this must have been!
The freedom of the unknown, the heaven of place.
The Micmacs who lived here learned the language of birds
Believing each shrill God's voice in the sky.
And often they'd come here just to pray for the fish,
To hear the echo of voices against these cliffs.

3
Naguset, Father of Day,
He made thunder sleep beneath the cliff,
He begot all creation the legend says.
In their shops the old women tell us again and again
How the Micmacs rose from soil like trees and flowers.

El'na, called Naguset, says the legend. *My People!*
The tide rushed in to nurse the foliage.
The moon swelled the breasts of the newborn mothers.
All this before the Jesuits claimed the land for France.
All this before the prophets ever spoke our names.

4
Nights by the cove make it easy to dream.
Plovers and gulls float overhead in the darkness,
Perch in a safe place only closed eyes can see.
When the breeze rises up from the mouth of the ocean
We give ourselves over to whatever will be.
Angel, come closer.

Let me feel your hair in a wide circle around me.
Let me feel the strength of your gentle hands.
For now let's be two ghosts stripped of our shadows,
Two bodies camouflaged in the shape of a flame.
The beauty of all things surrounds us
But only for as long as we can bear it.

5

Fifty miles south on the Fundy Bay
The big trawlers crawl back to St. John.
Steel cranes lift the nylon nets,
Rest them on scales, bury them in storage tanks
Where tonight they'll be frozen and by noon tomorrow
Shipped off to process on special trucks.

I don't hate those boats,
Not the oily decks or the grinding flywheels.
I don't hate the gift shops, the strip joints
Or even the drunk tourists honking their horns
To say Jesus loves them. Everything passes
And everything answers someone's prayer.

6

Awake again before the sun, we listen
To the waves recede, to the birds again
Spiraling up to heaven through morning fog.
Who'll tell us what to promise or to pray for?

What modest grace we can hope to earn?
Across the gulf the light expands
From eye to eye, the sun and moon trading place,
The world again ready to shed its human skin.
To a listening God we ask for nothing more
Than time and strength: Beg our own two hearts
For nothing less than the mercy of love.

II

After Harvest

If only you could believe in this:
That if some new thread of sunlight would curl
around the corn leaf it might all be different.
I know I'm groping. This morning
the air has no familiar scent.

In this field the last rows
of stubble are plowed back under.
The moist underside of soil is still warm.
Along the soles of my shoes confused insects
crawl through these mangled roots.

Tired of the road and tired of women
we pull off the highway six miles from Cleveland
for a minute's rest and a cup of coffee.
My brother's eyes are bloodshot.
His wife's left him and he hates himself
for being alone. For him I hate my own wife.
I hate myself for living with her.
We drink slowly without speaking, watching truckers
drive wheat toast through platters of eggs.
The soft eyes stare up and are eaten.
We think of the women they bring their bellies
home to; how they kiss and how they pass the time.
We try remembering how it was living alone before women.
My brother begins mumbling to himself.
I can barely watch him stir his coffee with his crooked spoon.
He rubs his eyes, remembering how it is to sleep alone.
I want to say, *Forget the bitch!*
She sucked you dry to the bone!
I want to say each hopeless lie a man could mumble to himself.
The waitress smiles bringing our check. She smells of grease
and we stink of sweat. I smile back. Outside the cold air
stings like some obscene kiss.
We've got an hour and a half until Toledo.
At the gas pump two girls are hitchhiking to Detroit.
One has hair like my wife's but smaller breasts.
We pause, watching diesels push their weight against the fog.

SUMMER ON GREEN LAKE

All summer we fished for bluegills, telling ourselves
we were fishing for bass. We guided our rowboat along the
     edge
of the weedbank, our poles like small branches alive in the
     wind.

Mornings were warm and humid. In the clear spaces between
     rocks
and weeds we tracked the small-mouths, their wide fins twisting
     coyly
away, their fertile bellies reflected in the small ripples of sun.

How we craved those sleek ones we never caught!
Others we knew we wouldn't eat we threw back.
Sailboats sailed by, their white sheets wide as the mouths of
     flowers.

In the hot afternoon we moved under trees bent over
the shore. Near the house we could see our wives playing cards
     on the lawn.
We remembered how the lake froze numb in winter.

At night we stopped rowing and gave ourselves over to drifting.
In the dark we heard the fish bob the surface for air
while the moon spread its fingers into the corners of the lake.

Oh the chances we gave ourselves on Green Lake, believing
   each day
we'd either catch the fish or forget them, believing
those dark beauties could be angled from their nests.

And each morning we'd lower the boat, our fingers moist
in the sun. And each night we'd raise it up again, cracked oars
and small leaks, our buckets still empty.

BENT TREE

I go a long way back to find that bent tree.
Alone in the middle of the garden, it had a knot
at its center, a small space where as a child
I imagined animals once lived.

How the time has passed since I tagged that tree,
lobbed rope over the branches and swung below
all summer long. Afternoons I'd fall off into deep dreams
and open my eyes to see the world, thick leaves
swimming above me in the wind like birds.

I remember years later looking for you in summer,
wondering where you might be on such a warm night.
Everything we loved had disappeared so fast.
And for nothing more than a fond thought I imagined you
beside that bent tree, your hair again long and
your skin so wild, chanting my name at the fat moon.

LAST WORDS AT MARBLEHEAD

We stood on a small mound near the lighthouse, alone
in gray fog, listening to saltwater slap the shore rocks beneath
    us.
I knew we would never be that lonely again.

Closer to the sand we listened to each other speak and listened
to the foam slide back through the pebble-bed. The sucking
made a dead sound, hollow as the wind that chased the gulls
    away.

We wanted an ache much deeper than our own.
We wanted a pain more fearful than forgetting. We wanted
the water to wrap us in its tongue, to teach us how to sleep.

Chilled and frightened you motioned me back to the car,
but I stood waiting, for a sign or a ghost, for a voice, for
    no one
but my unwilling self to stare out and turn away, to choose
    nothing over nothing.

In the Attic Where She Sleeps

1

In the attic where she sleeps
One by one I count the breaths,
Watch her chest ride up and down
The waves of dreams. Will she anchor

In a place where fathers live? I watch
How gently the night shapes itself around her.
I see too the world beyond her dreams.
Blood and water, warm leafy places.
Later, the crackle of sunlight on wood.

2

Daughter of mine
Where is the woman who loved you into being?
Who will teach you to draw, teach you
Not to live on the whims of desperate men?

3

Soft Egg, this darkness is your savior.
Wherever you go it will hide you,
Offer an ear for your fragile secrets.
Trust this hard silence.

Years from now when I have no shape
Talk to the darkness and I'll be listening.
When you are nothing to no one
Believe in it. Alone it will carry you
Back to a loving time.

FOR MY BROTHER: ON THE COURAGE OF BIRDS

For hours we'd admire the courage of birds,
Their infidelity to gravity,
That instinctive grace which leaves suffering
To the human hands that pray for it.

And each spring we'd watch them return,
Blue-winged warblers, yellow-breasted chats
And further north among the pine
The slate-colored juncos.
"Peterson" in our pockets we looked for subtle shades,
Sat for hours alone listening for the fragile truth.

The Fragile Truth!
How we pressed our ears to the wall of that wind.
How we prayed for some dignity beyond affection.
We longed for the courage to call ourselves men,
To ask nothing at all of the mouths of women.

Some years had passed when one by one
You cocked your gun and shot them. And didn't I watch
As one by one another followed in its place?
We were wrong, you said, about the courage of birds.
They fly wherever the wind demands,
Pawns of the seasons, prisoners of the sky.

Oh brother of mine, what is it
This need to love or suffer?
No longer young in my life

I fall victim to distraction,
I become pitifully dependent on the love of strangers.

Overhead now in a September sky
The spring birds circle too quick to name.
A slackened rope, they stretch out over the tops of trees
Become silhouettes in the silver lakes of clouds.
But those nests still warm in the naked crooks—
Even now I still stare at them with a wistful eye.
We were wrong about the courage of birds.
We were deaf and blind to the fragile truth.
Pawns of the seasons, prisoners of the sky . . .
And still they fly.

THE LONG NIGHTS OF WAITING

1

The moist peat rises up and circles
the dense leaves. These are the last days
before harvest, the long nights of waiting.
Love, can you hear the horses through your sleep
fighting for the last grain? Even the cows
in deep grass pound their hooves in the dark.
What new secret have they learned?
That in a month they'll be dead?
You can hear the flies buzz above their heads
in the patient blackness.

2

Soon it will be over.
The cows will be sold to slaughter
and these fields again will be nothing more
than mangled roots and stubble.
Nature never disappoints itself.
But what if we stay here through winter?
Take whatever it is that's made us lonely
and plow it back under? Covered in snow
these fields may be forgiving and
patience itself is a way of loving.

The Singing Between

1

If I've pitied the season helplessly dying
I've pitied myself. For what? You know,
these aches defy me but please believe
I never wanted this: The fear,
the spite, this hateful love.

In naked October the days are straining.
The sun can barely muster a light
through thinning trees. No smell
of salty summer. No kiss behind the knee.
Autumn's too quiet!
The warblers are tongue-tied in the red leaf.
Bluegills hug the bottom of the lake.
On the rusted fence even the crows huddle
in a choir of silence.

2

In the garden at Chartres, in front of the cathedral
old women sold their linens in the oily rain.
Slow shoes inched through the mud, both spires were lost in
    gray.
Each stony saint seemed to hide within his pleat.
Inside, the candlelight and dust made us feel like pilgrims.
A tour guide spoke in whispers:
Here is where the fire is believed to have started.
Those who managed to escape the flames were lost to smoke.

Do you remember? One stained glass was out to repair.
We heard a mass for true believers.
Can you remember now?
A voice in my chest prayed hard you'd stay.
Your eyes turned away to read the ancient scrawl.
When the train passed the walls shook
and our loneliness shook the walls.

3

What words could hold our secrets?
What logic understands desire?
You shamed me into loving,
made me feel empty and naked without you.

Night after night we rocked the floor
with our frantic breathing.
How we pitied the sad and tired world.
Yet now I see how everything tires,
how everything saddens until even happiness
tugs at the heart until it aches.
And ours was a blind ache stumbling
in the dark, a ripe appetite
for fire and despair.

4

When I think of you I think of water,
of rivers and seas and the Dutch canals.

Your eyes become fish in streams I have known.
I try not to remember the muddy corners, the dark eddies
or the low banks where the current sleeps with soot and mud.
I try remembering only what I can accept:

We were standing at the edge of a lake.
A black bass was sleeping near a cool rock.
Two bluegills were stealing someone's bait.
I'm lying.
It was the fourth of May.
I'm lying.
Small children splashed after minnows.
I'm lying.
The air was sweet. Your eyes were diamonds.
Your eyes were empty and the air repulsed you.

In a damp cafe we sat stupid from gin
watching rain wash the trolleys en route to the depot.
The clouds were bloodshot, old and European.
You stumbled home and made love to a stranger.
I woke up brittle, ugly and American.

        5
Year after year
the years become a cluttered wall,
the specifics generalized, the desires
permanent but always vague.

Even the days themselves, small prayers each
dissolve into a landscape of screams
and laughter racing backwards out of reach.
Please understand this ache.
Giving it up is no easy thing.

6

Already the first snow's here
and the first winter birds perch in the silence
of the patient trees. Not even a whisper
but I know they can sing.
They shake their heads and quiver their throats
to imitate me.

Under the moon tonight
I'll walk these fields and name each star
whose light I know.
I'll clear my throat and shape a sound
for all the birds to hear.
It's a song of love and forgiveness;
so if you can't hit the high notes
but can't hold your tongue
you can still sing between.
It's a song of regret and acceptance;
of choosing dreams over nightmares
and sleep over dreams.

Look how the snow dances
to the whim of the wind, how the last leaves
tear off and fly no longer rooted
in one perpetual place!
There's still time to walk before
the ice sets in. Still time,
I know, for all the birds to sing.

III

THE WOMAN IN THE DREAM

The woman in the dream came to me
like no one you could ever be. Cloud upon cloud
of black hair, it billowed like waterfall over her neck,
fell to a place on her spine I could feel with my eye.
Believe me when I tell you she promised me nothing.
And we walked and walked in a dreamless stride,
not through fields or pasture or some place by the water
where alewives shimmer in refracted light.
But through car lots and deserted brownstones,
the city's empty pockets, traffic noise
scratching our ears and the obscenity
of everything we loved clearly in front of us.

Suddenly we were among animals.
One chained dog, foaming and feverish,
gnawed to the bone the flesh of its paw
while somehow nearby, their eyes still intact,
the skins of sheep dried in the sun.
I wanted to run, to bolt away,
to hold my throat and spit my stomach into my shivering
     hands.
I was frightened by the blood and her unshaking calm.
But when I heard you weeping in the distance,
heard you praying for my safety, pleading like a child
for this night to end, I knew nothing we loved
could ever redeem me.

It was then that I begged for her scent.
In the midst of that suffering I wanted her sex

wrapped around me in a passion you can't even dream.
And as she pushed back her hair,
as she threw off her shawl and stepped out of her dress,
I heard your screams and took one last breath
of the nauseous decay; one arm pulling her close
as if embracing an angel.
The other reaching out willingly to the dog's rabid teeth.

RULES OF THE WEATHER

Heaven only knows what man
brings home the belly of his troubles to you.
Impatient always, you wait for him,
never quite sure what worlds he has to conquer,
what he dreams he must do to earn your love.
He lives by the rules of the weather:
Always respect what no one fears.

This is no world for crippled hearts,
for passion as desperate as a revelation or lie.
You watch him as he eats his food.
I've known men before, you think to yourself.
*It takes a lifetime to teach them
anything about love.*

The Angel on the Backyard Porch

All night he hears you singing,
hears that love song he thinks
only you can make him hear.
Angel, he calls and he is talking
to you, he is listening for your breeze
swimming through the chimes.

Surely you've seen men pray this way
before; surely you've heard them scream
for love slowly as fear demands.

This is the night of the equinox,
half a billion hearts balanced on a pin.
When morning coughs itself awake
he'll still be dreaming of worlds he finds you in.
He'll have memorized each word you sang
and croon them softly to a listening God.

With Emmylou Harris in Heaven

In Memory of David Holman

If he followed her on faith alone
then doubting God never destroyed his faith.
Take it or leave it heaven's alright,
he thinks to himself. Once you leave Texas
everything takes a little getting used to.

Mornings she likes to sleep in.
He takes his coffee and Pall Malls
to the front porch where inchworms stretch
in the sun. It's always the first day
of summer. Fat bees suck the lilacs
without modesty or hesitation.

If I stayed true to form, he thinks,
it would be easy to throw this all away,
to take everything for granted except
the weather. In Ft. Worth the sky's
just a calendar of sour luck. A man never
builds a house he can't bear to lose.

But later, when she sings to him about
Boulder and Birmingham, about grievous angels
and the patience of love he forgets how the dust
nearly choked his life. He remembers only
how her mouth taught his skin to sing.

Come midnight his cigarette glows
like a firefly when seen across the road,

appears a faint and distant star to all
who pray from earth. He has no words
to firm their faith in love, no shape
of hope for the poor to flatter.

From deep in the night he hears her
screech and howl, hears her bark
at the moon in a wicked fever.
Later he'll hold her until she cries
herself to sleep, soothe her lips
from the kiss of a jealous God.

NAKED

Only she knew how naked I was,
Nakedness being a matter of degree.
Even when I came back alone the only bones
Others saw were the ones I gave them to see.

For something less than love she kept
Our secret secret: How we sat in that Amsterdam bar
Drinking gin, she pretending I was more drunk
Than upset while I scribbled her words on a napkin.

Who'd have guessed my eyes would be so free?
I shivered at the word *alone.* "You're tired,"
She said. "Let's talk it over in the morning."
And sober, walked me back to our pension.

FROM THE PARIS HOTEL WINDOW

So long ago now
even memories can't be trusted,
I take comfort in facts: The year,

the place, the sweet yet unfamiliar taste
of a world by rite of love
we imagined we'd created.

Where else but Paris
to set our young hearts free? Kisses
along the Seine, sly glances at the moon,

that murderous desire to love everything;
to be a part of everything
that imagines itself beautiful.

And we *were* beautiful, weren't we?
You with your hungry eyes and wise hands,
me with my nervous schemes.

What a language of awkwardness we made
fumbling in the dark, laugh after laugh,
scream after rakish scream.

What happened then I can't remember.
The memories lose their place.
Two dogs raced the sidewalk chased

by the wind while lightning cursed
the sky in broken French,
pushing the moon back to America.

Love, what dream
were you dreaming that night?
Who was taking you away and where?

I watched your eyelids flitter
like restless wings as if wings alone
might free you from those lonely branches.

And toward morning,
my own prayer for wings unanswered,
I returned to our bed and your quiet skin:

Watching free clouds drift across the shifting sky.

A Note Found after the Storm

It's all right now.
The rain has stopped and I've started to clear
the scattered branches.
You lived here once and know how it is.
The rain waxed the new corn to mud
and when the wires fell the gate lit up
quivering like a fish nerve hooked clean under the gums.
I was frightened. I underestimated
the strength of the storm.
Face to face with those elephant clouds
I tried my best to fall in love with crashing shudders.
I became desperate with promises.
To the leaking roof I pledged allegiance
to all in heaven. To the pulsing glass
I swore I'd never break a heart.
I told myself if I made it through just one more time
I'd give it up for anything close to love or money.
You've said that to yourself many times.
But now the sky here is paling blue as a hyacinth
and the moon's disappeared to wherever it goes.
Things could have been worse.
The house itself is still in good shape
even those delicate things I keep inside.
Things are worse in some drier places.
Listen. You can hear the horses grumbling.
They know I can't promise it won't happen again,
that's how it is when you love a storm.

A blackbird just hopped on the dangling gate
bobbing his head like the wink of an eye.
What's he promising? Probably nothing.
Nothing, at least, he can't fly away from.

Your uncle is tired. Winter is no place for an old man to live.
The nights are too lonely. There is no money.
Some sheep have died of anthrax and the soil is cracked.
At night the wind moves in circles around the house.
Everything is dead or falling off to sleep.

      *

The snow never stops or so it seems. Can you who are so
    tender
know what it's like to feel so withered? Impatient days
are passed in boring deeds. The frozen air dares
you to breathe. Forgive me but I've been alone too long.

      *

Yelena and the Professor have arrived. Dr. Astrov too.
He drinks too much vodka. They say the czar is losing his
    mind.
I am better, thank you. I think too much and a touch
of consumption turns my head. You are precious to care.

      *

Sonia has fallen for Dr. Astrov. Poor girl,
she keeps an oil lamp burning by her bed all night.
And Yelena? Perhaps you remember how beautiful she is.
Her eyes are like the blue heart of a flame.
As for the Professor . . . I'll be kind. He busies himself
with busy work ("a biography of Pushkin," he says).
I'm enjoying the intrusion of other voices.

*

Have I told you what lunacy Dr. Astrov speaks?
Workers owning land and other such nonsense.
Vodka can be a dangerous vice. Some nights he swears
he hears angels. Poor Dr. Astrov.
Not even forty and a fool already.

*

The season turns slowly but it turns. The sun rises now
before the animals. We live on little more than biscuits
but I am happier. Poor Sonia still suffers silently.
And Yelena, ah Yelena. She's touched me in a place
I can't tell. She makes me dream and dreaming is not easy
     here.
What can I say? Love in the heart of an old man stirs dust.

*

Finally spring is here. The first buds stare off the trees
like infant's eyes, soft and pale, unaware of their becoming.
Something in spring makes me think I could move beyond
     the past.
The air is so wet and sweet. If only I had faith.
If only I could paint I would walk outside into the field
and sketch a closing door behind me.

*

Yelena! Yelena! What other name should I know?
Yelena the beautiful. Yelena the untouchable.

Even her voice tears me all ways. She's too young
to be married to such a parasite, such a fraud
as the Professor (who cares who Pushkin loved?).
I could show her what a man really is.
What stops me from loving her? What?
My Honor? Her honor?
Honor is a word for dreamers invented by Shakespeare.

    *

What a fool! What an idiot!
Yelena has played me for a child. I caught her with Dr. Astrov
in the garden (my own garden no less!). I could smell
the passion curling around them like a snake.
Everything is filth. Everything dirt.
I should have shot them both like field rats.
I am too old to nurse a broken heart.
What will I do when my rage turns to desolation?

    *

Sonia says I have disgraced the family. I have thrown
them all out—Astrov, Yelena, the Professor. Sent them all
    packing.
They are lucky to have left alive.
Even now when the sun lifts the rain from morning grass
I feel no remorse. My only pangs are for Sonia.
She is so young and opens her heart to thieves.

*

Summer's moved too quickly and already the evenings are cool.
The shrill of the cicada is fading and the crickets rub
their dry wings under rocks. A modest crop may sustain us.
I wonder what keeps old men from telling the truth?
I am remembering how it is to age.
Even poor Sonia spends hours watching the leaves turn.
My dearest niece and nephew, listen to your sad uncle.
All change comes too quickly but perhaps
this is better than no change.
Sonia has faith and I have will. If our hands are busy
we have nothing to fear from the long nights.
Be well and kind to one another.

IV

SECRETS OF SUCCESS

1

The money I learned to love myself
for as little as there was to learn.
From my father I learned how to fail
and survive, how to succeed without joy.
It takes a man with a future to see
that desperation's a verb in any language
including love.

2

All night it helps me sleep to know
the cars are safe, the house insured
and my wife's new clothes will not
jeopardize the mortgage. I find
courage in the sure fist of bonds.
Charities court my thoughtfulness.
Lenders respect my earning power,
my capacity for achievement and regret.

3

Being neither rich nor poor I don't have
the luxury of an open mind to guide me.
I measure my manhood against the crack
of the wishbone, against envy and desire
and the wind into which even lesser men spit.
I put myself above nothing and no one:
Not murder, not mercy, not even the love
of a dangerous God.

OZONE PARK, 1955

There's no mistaking these streets,
row after row of identical soldiers except
for the painted aluminum doors.
Another "dream neighborhood" for anyone
who survived Europe and Korea
and could afford not to see themselves
as crippled or confused.
There was hope in that confusion,
queasy hope that things had somehow
just gotten out of hand like some teenage
party with too much beer.
We were the children of that inheritance,
the bandage conceived to hide the wounds
and keep the leaky stuff inside.
We did our best.
Ralph Montenaro gave a spit-shine
you could shave in. Larry Jacobs could punch
a Spalding past three city sewers.
Even little "Perspiration Pete" who'd soak
his pants in mid-sentence could make you
scream when he pulled his ears
and said, "What me worry?"
His mother was president of the P.T.A.
She said it was the communists who
put fluoride in the water.

OTTO FRANK AT NINETY-ONE

He knows that's the trouble with most old men.
What they dream and what they've done
gets scratched by the same uneasy hand.
Not Otto Frank. His memory is the blood of hard wood.
His fate is splitting the nightmares from the dreams.

Imagine a storm in the night, sirens
in the street, voices pleading with a moon
seduced by thunder: *Nightmare.*
Years later his ears can still separate
which sounds came through the door or window,
the snap of bones or branches, a howl in the night
from the dog or the dead.

This morning he'll wake again surprised,
spread his crumbs and answer the birds who steal
his sleep. No longer frightened they peck his hand,
measure each line with the peaceful eyes
he's seen in dreams. *Or were they dreams?*
The smoke and sulphur? Love as a word that's cut
from your tongue and sewn to your feet?

Lifting one sparrow against the sky
he forces himself to remember everything:
The dancing reeds around the lake,
the blossoming sap in the veins of children,
that paradise so long abandoned which God himself
once promised us.

A KADDISH FOR VICTOR KUGLER

God the painter contemplated everything
he could not create and grew disgusted.
Our tall prayers aside,
it was not the universe he longed for
but his own face which he'd never seen.

For centuries he sat in the dark room
of nothing and dreamed.
He dreamed his eyes as ocean,
his nose as rock, his mouth a cavern
of light and wet from which all joy
might shape a sound.

But God the painter had no joy
and he had no love
that didn't long for his own face.
The wind which was his blood
crashed east and west against itself,
churned north and south
in the slow twist of time.

Victor! Victor Kugler!
What would you teach us now?
That God the painter was the author
of fate not its master? His own portrait
too accurate, too selfish,
thriving as we know on adoration
and pain?

Or free now from this twisted canvas
would you insist instead we not leave
the painter to his own self-hate?
That we trust at last in the true life
of art and go off in search of the very wings
God himself could not find.

Victor Kugler was the Dutch spice merchant in whose attic Anne
Frank and her family hid from the Nazis for twenty-five months.
A devout Christian, he was sent to the death camps himself but
managed to escape. He later emigrated to Canada, where he died
in 1981.

A Papal Mass at Auschwitz
Forty Years after the Holocaust
June 8, 1979

> I have said to corruption,
>   thou art my father; to the worm,
>   thou art my mother, and my sister.
> —Job 17:14

It's safe now as you know.
Bodies no longer burn the rain.
No one will scar your face
just to eat your shoe. Say a prayer,
nobody's hungry here.

Forty years ago now
the first boxcars rolled in. If you
sleep with both of your ears
to the ground Jesus will tell you
how hard it is to raise

mismatched bones from the grave.
Believe him. Every Pole and Jew
bulldozed under your feet
took root like some forgotten weed.
From underneath they claw

the heaven of your shoe.
Can you feel the itch the spider
scratches for them? It's here,
in the loins, where desire gnaws
the dead wood. Pray for them,

for their lost souls below,
for their faith knotted on the corm.
Their seeds have now risen
to our world above. They watch us
from the leafy branches.

Bless the soft hearts of ants,
the mole's flat stare and bad breath.
Pray for the grinning soul
of Mengele, for the twins sewn
together at the eyes.

V

For Poppa, Asleep in the Smithtown Madhouse

When they knew you were sick
you drove yourself nuts. Chasing nurses
for crazy laughs, chewing through ashtrays
just to prove you were insane.
Hardening of the arteries, they said.
You squealed your approval
tugging at your open fly.

Lonely Ruth who washed her hair with beer
said you chased her into the bathroom.
Maybe she hated you for being the father
of her husband who was the father of her sons.
Maybe she hated the disease of men, her mother dying
and her own father in the streets with his linens and his ladies.
No matter. She washed and washed but the pain wouldn't
    rinse.
You son of a bitch stay away from me, she screamed.
Some days you were there, other days you were sleeping.
This day your stomach growled. Your idiot hunger
pressed hard against the door.

The year was 1955
and what you needed Poppa was a good guess.
Every lawn was green with fluoride
and heaven so close we all begged to die.
At Smithtown you said it's better this way
but you were talking to the moon, talking to the blue face
of a young wife a million years ago.

Later, starving yourself to pneumonia
you cried, *No more, no more.*
I don't want to dream.

Oh Poppa, Poppa, bless me a voice.
I'm living with my own dreams now, clutching
wind through grass as if something could be saved.
I'm exhausted by the stubborn tick of possibility.
Still, when I take a deep breath from the fog of your face,
see your gray cap floating like a windy cloud,
it somehow seems right despite this madhouse.
Even riding in that old Nash one last time
you forgave them, didn't you?
A giant hand reached to tousle my hair
while I held my tears like a little man.
That wind I'm clutching says you forgave me too.

POPPA TOURS THE SMITHTOWN MADHOUSE

This driveway is the heaven you never expected.
Long as your patience, curved soft as a schoolgirl's calf.
You can smell the rain these enormous pines hold
for hours after. Memorize that smell.
It will come in handy should you forget your name
or if the emerald grass should make you think
it's always Christmas. It's never Christmas
unless they plug in the lights between your ears.

If today is Sunday there'll be a picnic.
We'll eat fried chicken and scatter the bones like flowering
     seeds.
Here in this field you're free to wander, free to dream
yourself whatever you dream. This is the new medicine.
The lunatics are still kept locked out of sight
but *softwares* like you can chase the clouds all summer.
Don't be frightened. Don't try to jump that fence around your
     brain.
You're expected back for lunch, for pills, for shots and dinner.

. . . Here is where we sit when the evenings come,
when the crickets shine in wet grass and a tired fog
wraps the moon in gauze. Make yourself comfortable in the possibil-
     ity of all things.
Two Lucky Strikes and all your hours begin again: Russian names,
     woolen dresses.
The smell of fish and hot manure steam up from cobblestone streets.
That's it, relax. Give yourself over to the slow peeling of rust.

There you are fierce and handsome, straining your way up walkups,
delivering your fabric to the chatter of stitching.
Down by the cart you bend and squat, dragging the twined bundles
onto your back, the fist between your legs tightening as you stand.
Day after day, step after step, did you ever think heaven
was just another flight up? That if you found it someone, somehow
would know enough to come and lead the horses home?
Eugene! Eugene! Tender voices called to you,
but you were too busy, your back was turned and when you finally
looked around here you were at Smithtown staring at the sun.
If you give your ears to the right wind you'll hear your name again.
You'll hear the horses too, slabbering their bits
and tail-swatting flies, patient in the narrow street.

When the last door locks this is where we sleep.
Toe to toe, east and west. Don't mind the black boys
and they won't mind you so long as you don't wet the bed.
Listen: This is the place where time stops running out.
Things you did and never thought about
become the things you think and never do.
Listen: A hard wind is twisting through the summer trees.
If you hear a scream keep your mouth shut tight until it
    disappears.
The branches bend, the branches shake,
but once they crack nothing hurts.

POPPA PRAYS AT SMITHTOWN
BUT TO WHOM HE DOESN'T KNOW

What can I tell my bones?
They stare out at me from inside.
"What unholy dreams did you have?" they ask.
Dreams, I shout, what dreams?
Inside I hear a brittle clatter.
Outside I hear old birds singing.
Are they the same birds as last year?
Have I been asleep so long?
Sssh. Stop your crying. Others are sleeping.
An old man's voice is calling from my bed.
Sonny, what does he want?
Angels? A bedpan?
Give him some water, something to eat.
Better, give him a woman to help him sleep.
And not the wrinkled ones who cry by the window.
Give him the one in the white dress,
With the big tits and shaved legs.
Damn it give him something or let him die!
Sssh. Stop your crying. This will help you sleep.
What happens now nobody knows.
Everything smells like spoiled milk.
Meyer, that bastard, you couldn't trust him!
I know, I know, it's time to sleep.
Stop him, that butcher, he murdered my wife!
Where are my pants? Who stole my pants?
Everything smells like spoiled milk.
I know, I know, it's time to sleep.

WAITING FOR POPPA AT THE SMITHTOWN DINER

1

Strangely enough something's still here.
Not the same modest caterpillar with red vinyl booths
but something, someplace you can come twenty years later
and whisper, *Long ago I knew this life.*
You'd know it in a second Poppa. You'd track each smell
and find your seat long before you'd recognize me.

Every other Sunday we loaded the Nash
with toothpaste and cigarettes to visit you. At Smithtown
the grounds were trim but your white scruff always bristled.
Looking up, your cap was a half-moon
I dreamed of touching.
This is what I've lived to remember
and what you killed yourself to forget.

2

On paper it never looked good, Poppa.
Facts can't always barter with time for sympathy.
Yours was a world of dresses and deliveries,
of satin and syphilis and whores who purred like wives
in the rabid eyes of your desire.
One by one dying aunts cursed your name:
You killed your wife with neglect, they said.
They cursed your name but they loved your money.
The locked their doors and made you pay
to see their children. Years later,
half-crazy and shamed into madness

you peered down at nurses over toilet doors,
starving yourself to silence.

3

Two miles south that madhouse
rises out of nothing and there's nothing
frightening for the sane mind to see.
Spruce pines swirl up like cypress, black squirrels
play roulette with the bald teeth of tires.
It is a quiet so perfect owls claw themselves awake.

4

Help me, Poppa. Tell me
what loneliness infected your life.
Was it the frail wife dead at thirty-one?
The unnamed son the doctors stole away
or is it just the seed? The sour blood
of an unhealed wound inside your heart?

I'm listening, Poppa. My own heart
can't be trusted. I see you across this table now
but a different ghost answers each time
I speak your name.

5

By summer of '60 what a mess you were;
screaming at radios, swallowing cigarettes.
The ache of dry had powdered your brain.

Your face was a canvas stretched on metal bones.
Pneumonic spiders crawled through your lungs.
Nothing could come between you and your dying.

6

When the numb ice melts and water
is set free again the process continues;
the frail and unforgiven roots are swept away.
All else must clench the mud and suck
its way to blinding greenness.

Tug at me gently, Poppa.
High or low I want to know
you're always there within the water.

Here in this photograph
you're lifting me up high into the clouds
of your crazy weather.
Off to the side your children are mannequins
frozen in their shameful secrets.
But you're whispering to me in a painless voice,
our own secret, Poppa,
which I can just now hear.

POETRY FROM ILLINOIS

History Is Your Own Heartbeat
Michael S. Harper (1971)

The Foreclosure
Richard Emil Braun (1972)

The Scrawny Sonnets and
Other Narratives
Robert Bagg (1973)

The Creation Frame
Phyllis Thompson (1973)

To All Appearances: Poems New
and Selected
Josephine Miles (1974)

The Black Hawk Songs
Michael Borich (1975)

Nightmare Begins Responsibility
Michael S. Harper (1975)

The Wichita Poems
Michael Van Walleghen (1975)

Images of Kin: New and
Selected Poems
Michael S. Harper (1977)

Poems of the Two Worlds
Frederick Morgan (1977)

Cumberland Station
Dave Smith (1977)

Tracking
Virginia R. Terris (1977)

Riversongs
Michael Anania (1978)

On Earth as It Is
Dan Masterson (1978)

Coming to Terms
Josephine Miles (1979)

Death Mother and Other Poems
Frederick Morgan (1979)

Goshawk, Antelope
Dave Smith (1979)

Local Men
James Whitehead (1979)

Searching the Drowned Man
Sydney Lea (1980)

With Akhmatova at the Black Gates
Stephen Berg (1981)

Dream Flights
Dave Smith (1981)

More Trouble with the Obvious
Michael Van Walleghen (1981)

The American Book of the Dead
Jim Barnes (1982)

The Floating Candles
Sydney Lea (1982)

Northbook
Frederick Morgan (1982)

Collected Poems, 1930~83
Josephine Miles (1983)

The River Painter
Emily Grosholz (1984)